J
799
.24625
MAR

Martin, Michael

Pheasant hunting

EDGE BOOKS

⊙∘⟶ THE GREAT OUTDOORS ⟵∘⊙

PHEASANT HUNTING

Revised and Updated

by Michael Martin

Consultants:
Cheryl Riley, Vice President
Rich Wissink, Youth Programs Specialist
Pheasants Forever

Capstone
press®

Mankato, Minnesota

Edge Books are published by Capstone Press,
151 Good Counsel Drive, P.O. Box 669, Mankato, Minnesota 56002.
www.capstonepress.com

Library of Congress Cataloging-in-Publication Data
Martin, Michael, 1948–
    Pheasant hunting / by Michael Martin.—Rev. and updated.
    p. cm.—(Edge Books. The great outdoors.)
    Includes bibliographical references and index.
    ISBN-13: 978-1-4296-0823-7 (hardcover)
    ISBN-10: 1-4296-0823-4 (hardcover)
    1. Pheasant shooting—Juvenile literature. I. Title. II. Series.
SK325.P5M37 2008
799.2'4625—dc22   2007010773

Describes the activity of pheasant hunting, its equipment, skills, and safety guidelines.

Editorial Credits
Carrie Braulick, editor; Katy Kudela, photo researcher; Jenny Krueger, revised edition
    editor; Thomas Emery, revised edition designer; Kyle Grenz, revised edition
    production designer

Photo Credits
Capstone Press/Gary Sundermeyer, 13, 14, 19
Gary Kramer, 5, 11, 41
Henry F. Zeman, 28, 33
Hulton/Archive Photos, 7
iStockphoto, 27
Leonard Rue Enterprises, 36
Mark Raycroft, 31 (all)
Rob and Ann Simpson, 23
Shutterstock/Jeff Banke, cover
Todd W. Patrick Photography, 20, 43
Thomas Brownold, 24, 34, 39
Unicorn Stock Photos/Paula J. Harrington, 44; Tom Edwards, 9;
William H. Mullins, 17

1 2 3 4 5 6 12 11 10 09 08 07

TABLE OF CONTENTS

Essential content terms are highlighted and are defined at the bottom of the page where they first appear.

Chapter 1

PHEASANT HUNTING

Learn about the history of pheasant hunting and different kinds of pheasants.

P heasants are one of the most popular game birds in North America. People hunt these birds for food and recreation. Pheasants live throughout much of the United States and in parts of Canada.

History of Pheasant Hunting

Pheasants are not native to North America. They originally lived in Asia, Europe, and Japan. In the late 1800s, people brought pheasants to North America from other countries.

The first pheasants in North America were from China. In the early 1880s, a judge named Owen Denny bought eight pheasants at a Chinese market. He shipped the birds to his home in Oregon. But the birds died soon after their arrival.

Other popular birds for hunting include the American woodcock, quail, and ruffed grouse.

Denny then shipped about 50 birds to the United States. These birds survived the trip from China. Denny released the birds in Willamette Valley in northwestern Oregon. The birds' population rapidly grew. People first hunted them in 1892. Hunters killed more than 50,000 pheasants that year. In the early 1900s, people in other states and Canadian provinces brought pheasants to North America.

These non-native pheasant species mated with each other in North America, creating hybrids. This mixture of species was called a ring-necked pheasant. Today, ring-necked pheasants are the most commonly hunted pheasants.

About Pheasants

All pheasants are upland game birds. These birds live on land and stay in the same area year-round.

Pheasants have a wide range in North America. They live from southern parts of Canada to southern states such as

species—a specific type of plant or animal

hybrid—the offspring of two different species

The growth of the pheasant population led to a great deal of hunting in the early 1900s.

Oklahoma, New Mexico, and Texas. The largest U.S. pheasant populations are in Iowa, South Dakota, Nebraska, and Kansas. In Canada, Alberta, Saskatchewan, and Manitoba have the largest pheasant populations.

EDGE FACT ⟿⟋⟍

A pheasant habitat must supply food, water, shelter, and space for year-round survival.

Pheasants can live in a wide variety of habitats. Pheasants often live in fields, grassy ditches, and on prairies. They also live at the edges of wetlands and woodlands.

Pheasants eat a variety of foods. Some studies report that pheasants eat more than 500 different kinds of food. Grains, seeds, and insects make up most of their diet.

Ring-Necked Pheasants

Ring-necked pheasants receive their name from the white ring around the rooster's neck. Roosters are male pheasants. Female pheasants are called hens. It is legal to hunt only roosters in most areas of North America. This law helps maintain pheasant populations.

Ring-necked roosters share certain features. They are brightly colored. They have gray, blue, black, brown, and gold feathers on their bodies. A red patch circles each eye. Roosters also have shiny blue-green heads and yellow beaks. They have long tails. Some ring-necked roosters' tails are more than 2 feet (.6 meters) long.

habitat—the natural place and conditions where a plant or animal lives

The average lifespan of a ring-necked pheasant in the wild is 10 to 20 months.

Hens have features that are different from roosters. They have brown bodies with tan spots. A hen's tail is shorter than that of a rooster. It usually is less than 1 foot (.3 meter) long.

Chapter 2

EQUIPMENT

Learn about equipment, including shotguns, shells, and proper clothing.

H unters walk long distances, so they need equipment to stay comfortable and safe. They also need certain supplies to shoot pheasants.

Shotguns

Pheasant hunters use shotguns. These guns hold plastic cases called shells. The shells are located in a space in front of the trigger called a chamber. Shells contain gunpowder and small pellets made of steel or lead. These pellets are called shot.

Gunpowder creates an explosive charge when a hunter fires a shotgun. The charge pushes the pellets out of the gun's barrel. This long metal tube is located at the front of a gun.

Shotguns have different gauges. A gun's gauge is the inside width of its barrel. Most shotgun gauges are measured in millimeters. Common shotgun gauges for pheasant hunting are the 12-gauge, the 16-gauge, and the 20-gauge. Guns with low gauges are more powerful than guns with high gauges.

Most pheasant hunters use shotguns with short barrels. These barrels are usually 20 to 26 inches (51 to 66 centimeters) long. Standard shotguns may have barrels that are 28 to 30 inches (71 to 76 centimeters) long. Shotguns with short barrels are easier to carry and shoot than guns with long barrels.

Shot

Shot spreads out after it leaves the barrel. Usually, several pieces of shot must hit a pheasant to kill it.

Shot comes in different sizes. Most pheasant hunters use shot sizes from 2 to 7. Shot with a low number is larger than shot with a high number. For example, number 4 shot is larger than number 7 shot. Large shot

travels farther than small shot. It can often kill a pheasant that is more than 40 yards (37 meters) away. Small shot can kill a pheasant within about 35 yards (32 meters). But shells with large shot contain fewer pellets than shells with small shot. Hunters who use large shot have less of it available to hit a pheasant.

Essential Equipment

Legend

1. Warm clothing
2. Shotgun
3. Shells
4. First aid kit
5. Snacks
6. Orange hat
7. Map
8. Sturdy Shoes
9. Sunscreen
10. Compass
11. Hunting Vest

Many governmental agencies require hunters to use non-toxic shot on land owned by the government. This shot is made of metal such as steel, iron, or tin. These metals are not poisonous to birds. In the past, birds such as ducks were poisoned when they ate lead shot that had fallen on the ground.

Clothing

Pheasant hunters need to dress properly for the weather. Pheasant hunting seasons occur during fall. Because temperatures and weather conditions vary during fall, hunters should dress in layers. They then can add or remove clothing to keep themselves comfortable. The first clothing layer should keep hunters' skin dry. Hunters may wear synthetic fabrics for this layer. They often choose clothing made of polyester or polypropylene. Both polyester and polypropylene absorb moisture from the skin.

Hunters should wear wool or fleece clothing for the second layer. Fleece is soft and warm. Wool keeps pheasant hunters warm even when it becomes wet.

synthetic—made by people rather than found in nature

Outside Clothing Layer

Pheasant hunters' outside layer of clothing should resist wind and water. Hunters often wear a strong, smooth material called nylon for this layer. Nylon can also prevent burrs or thorns from sticking to or scratching hunters.

Hunters should wear blaze orange or red clothing over their outside clothing layer. Bright colors help hunters see each other. Many hunters wear blaze orange vests. These vests have pockets to hold shells and a pouch to carry dead pheasants. In cold weather, pheasant hunters should wear heavy jackets, hats, and gloves to keep warm.

Footwear

Pheasant hunters need sturdy, comfortable footwear. They sometimes walk near marshes or in snow. Hunters' boots should be lightweight and have waterproof rubber soles. The boots should reach past hunters' ankles. This length can help keep feet dry.

Many states and provinces require pheasant hunters to wear orange.

Other Equipment

Below are a few other items that pheasant hunters should carry with them.

- **Drinking Water**—at least 1 quart (.95 liters) of drinking water for every 5 miles (8 kilometers) you plan to walk

- **Extra Water**—for hunting dogs

- **High-Energy Snacks**—such as peanuts, beef jerky, or granola

- **Map**—of the hunting area, and a compass

- **Pocketknife**—to clean dead pheasants. Hunters use pocketknives to separate the pheasant meat from the internal organs. They then take out the meat.

Baked Pheasant

Serves: 4   *Children should have adult supervision.*

Ingredients:

4 boneless pheasant breasts
1 10.5-ounce (298-gram) can
  cream of chicken soup
½ cup (125 mL) apple cider
1 tablespoon (15 mL)
  Worcestershire sauce
¾ teaspoon (3 mL) salt

⅓ cup (75 mL) chopped onion
1 clove minced garlic
1 3-ounce (13-gram) can of
  mushrooms (drained)
1 teaspoon (5 mL) paprika
3 tablespoons (45 mL) apricot jam
½ teaspoon (2 mL) ground ginger

Equipment:

9- by 9-inch (23- by 23-centimeter)
  square baking pan
Medium bowl

Mixing spoon
Small bowl
Spatula

1. Heat oven to 350°F (180°C). Place pheasant breasts in baking
   pan.

2. Mix soup, cider, Worcestershire sauce, salt, onions, garlic,
   and mushrooms together in medium bowl. Pour over pheasant.

3. Sprinkle both sides of pheasant generously with paprika. Mix
   jam and ground ginger together in small bowl. Bake pheasant
   1½ to 2 hours. Use spatula to spread part of jam mixture over
   pheasant after about ½ hour. Turn pheasant over after about
   1 hour. Spread jam mixture over other side of pheasant.

20 Sunglasses and a cap with a brim help protect a pheasant hunter's eyes.

First Aid Kit

Hunters should also carry a first aid kit. These kits usually include scissors, tweezers, gauze, and adhesive bandages. First aid kits also have cream to protect wounds from germs. Hunters can use the same cream for wounds on dogs. Hunting dogs can become injured if they run through thick or thorny plant growth.

Chapter 3

SKILLS AND TECHNIQUES

Learn about shooting techniques, hunting alone and in groups, and dogs used in hunting.

Pheasant hunting involves a lot of skill. Hunters should know where to look for pheasants. They also need to know proper shooting techniques.

Drive Hunting

Many hunters drive pheasants. Hunters who use this technique form a line and slowly walk across a field. They move toward another line of hunters located at the other end of the field. These hunters are called blockers. The walking hunters startle pheasants, who then move toward the blockers.

Pheasants often flush when they come within about 50 yards (46 meters) of the blockers. Hunters make pheasants flush so they can see the pheasants clearly before shooting.

flush—to fly up and out of cover

Pheasant hunters who drive should walk closely together.

Pheasant hunters who use the drive method should walk closely together. Pheasants may move through gaps between hunters.

Hunters who drive need to be careful. Both hunters and blockers must decide who will shoot at the birds. They must also decide in which directions they will shoot. Walkers and blockers must not shoot toward one another.

Hunting Alone and Small Group Hunting

Many people hunt pheasants alone or in small groups. These hunters usually look for pheasants in small areas. These areas include small fields, ditches, or marsh edges. Lone hunters or hunters in small groups walk through their hunting areas. They usually try to force pheasants into areas with few hiding places.

Lone hunters and hunters in small groups should walk slowly. Pheasants often do not flush if hunters move too quickly. Because pheasants can hear well, hunters should talk as little as possible. Pheasants often run away from noisy hunters. Some hunters use hand signals to communicate instead of talking.

Pheasant hunters with dogs usually try to walk into the wind. The wind will then blow a pheasant's scent toward a dog.

Some pheasant hunters zigzag across open areas or stop for a few moments. The birds are then more likely to hide until a hunter comes near them. Hunters want pheasants to flush within shooting range.

Hunting Dogs

Hunters who use trained dogs are able to find and shoot more pheasants. With amazing skill, hunting dogs help locate and retrieve birds. For more information on hunting dogs, see page 30.

Shooting

Pheasant hunters must learn how to hit moving targets. Hunters often use the swing-through technique to shoot pheasants. Hunters hold the shotgun with one hand behind the trigger. They place the other hand underneath the gun's forestock. This part is located underneath the back end of the barrel.

28 Hunters should always know where members in their own party, as well as other hunters and hunting dogs are.

The hand under the forestock raises the barrel. The other hand brings the end of the gun to the shoulder. Hunters then swing the gun's barrel in front of the flushing pheasant. This action is called "leading." Hunters sometimes need to lead several feet in front of pheasants. Hunters should continue to move the barrel as they pull the trigger.

Hunters should shoot only at birds within shooting range, aiming for the bird's upper body. If birds are injured but not killed, they might escape and suffer before they die.

Hunters should watch where pheasants land after they shoot them. Injured birds may run away. Hunters should try to find every bird that they shoot.

Hunting dogs help tremendously in the field, and they're companions on and off the hunt. Dogs are at an advantage when it comes to hunting. Unlike people, dogs can easily smell pheasants. Dogs called pointers signal to hunters that the birds are nearby. Other dogs flush the pheasants so the hunters can see where they are.

Hunting dogs can also remember where the birds fall, and retrieve them for the hunter. They can prevent wounded birds from escaping.

A properly trained pheasant hunting dog is amazingly obedient and loyal. Following commands at a distance and approaching a hunt with unbounded enthusiasm make hunting dogs a favorite part of the sport.

EDGE FACT

Some extreme breeds such as poodles are also used as Pheasant Hunting dogs!

English Springer Spaniel

English springer spaniels originally came from Great Britain. They are about 20 inches (51 centimeters) tall. Their name comes from the way they spring forward to flush birds. People once called English springer spaniels Norfolk spaniels. These dogs are black and white or brown and white. English springer spaniels have long, drooping ears. They have medium to long coats.

German Short-Haired Pointer

People brought German short-haired pointers to North America from Germany in the 1920s. These dogs range from 21 to 25 inches (53 to 64 centimeters) tall. German short-haired pointers have a muscular build and a short back. They usually are solid brown, brown and white, or black and white. They have short, coarse coats.

English Setter

English setters are originally from Great Britain. They usually are 24 to 26 inches (61 to 66 centimeters) tall. Their flat, thick coats are mainly white. They often have small markings called flecks. These flecks may be black, tan, yellow, brown, or orange. English setters often have wavy hair on their ears, chest, legs, underbody, and tail. Their long, rounded ears are set low on their head.

Chapter 4

CONSERVATION

Learn about Pheasants Forever, conservation efforts, and hunting regulations.

In the 1960s and 1970s, pheasant populations declined in the United States. Farmers used much of pheasants' habitat to grow crops. Some people mowed or burned roadside ditches. Hens had fewer safe areas to hide their nests from predators. Skunks, raccoons, and snakes ate pheasant eggs before the young could hatch.

Pheasants Forever

In 1982, a group of Minnesota hunters formed an organization called Pheasants Forever. The group's main goal was to protect and restore pheasant habitat.

Today, more than 115,000 North Americans are members of Pheasants Forever. Through its more than 600 chapters, the organization also has a strong youth education program.

34 Pheasant hunters often hunt in grassy CRP areas.

Pheasants Forever develops pheasant habitat in several ways. It pays farmers to plant grasses. The group buys land to establish pheasant habitat. It also restores wetlands. People sometimes drain wetlands to build houses or other buildings.

The CRP

In 1985, the U.S. government passed the Conservation Reserve Program (CRP). The CRP program pays farmers if they do not grow crops in certain areas. The program's purpose is to improve water quality, support wildlife, and prevent soil erosion. Soil that erodes or wears away can prevent the land from producing quality crops. The soil can also enter water sources. Chemicals in the soil then can pollute these water sources.

EDGE FACT ⟶⌀⌀

Pheasants Forever has developed more than 3 million acres (1.2 million hectares) of pheasant habitat since its beginning.

soil erosion—the wearing away and movement of soil

36 CRP areas help keep recently hatched pheasants safe from predators.

The federal government also pays farmers to plant grasses in CRP areas. These areas provide hens with good nesting cover. The CRP areas have greatly increased pheasant habitat in many parts of the United States.

Regulations

Today, North American pheasant populations are large. Millions of pheasants live in North America. But hunters still need to follow state and provincial regulations to maintain these populations.

State and provincial government agencies study the number of pheasants in certain areas. They then set a limit. The limit is the number of pheasants hunters can kill and take home in one day. In most states and provinces, hunters have limits of between two and four roosters. Agencies may allow hunters to kill more pheasants in places with large pheasant populations.

Government agencies also set seasons. Pheasant hunting season usually begins in October. The season's length depends on the area's pheasant population. In most areas, the season lasts between three and ten weeks.

Agencies set other regulations. All hunters of a certain age need to buy a license. This minimum age is between 16 and 18 in most areas. Younger hunters must hunt with an adult.

Regulations may require hunters to leave certain parts of a dead pheasant intact for identification. Agency workers sometimes check to make sure hunters have a pheasant and not another type of bird. For example, pheasant hunters may need to leave at least one leg and one foot or the head on each dead pheasant.

EDGE FACT ──◦·☺

In some areas, pheasant hunters must buy conservation stamps. Agencies use the money they receive for the stamps to improve or establish pheasant habitat.

Young hunters should hunt with an adult.

Chapter 5

SAFETY

Learn about gun safety, first aid, and recognizing poisonous plants.

All pheasant hunters should plan for a safe hunt. Some hunters take safety courses to learn proper hunting practices. Government agencies and hunting organizations offer these courses.

Gun Safety

Hunters must follow basic gun safety rules. They should not point their gun at another person or anything that they do not mean to shoot. Hunters should make sure they can see the target clearly. They must be sure the area beyond their target is clear. Hunters should unload guns after they finish using them and always store guns unloaded. Hunters must also keep the shotgun's safety on at all times except when shooting.

safety—a device located near the trigger that prevents a gun from firing

Other Safety Concerns

Pheasant hunters should follow other safety guidelines. All hunters should have basic first aid skills. Hunters should check the weather forecast before their trip. They need to stay aware of changing weather conditions. A snowstorm or heavy rain can make it difficult for hunters to see.

Hunters should recognize plants growing in their hunting areas. Thorny plants sometimes grow in pheasant habitats. Certain plants can cause a skin rash. These plants include poison ivy, poison oak, and poison sumac.

Safe pheasant hunters avoid dangerous situations. They know that responsible behavior will reduce accidents and help keep their sport enjoyable.

Safe pheasant hunters stay aware of their surroundings at all times.

The Ring-Necked Pheasant

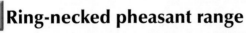
Ring-necked pheasant range

Description: Ring-necked pheasants usually are 30 to 36 inches (76 to 91 centimeters) long. They weigh from 2 to 5 pounds (.9 to 2.3 kilograms). Rooster ring-necked pheasants are brightly colored birds with long tails. They have a mixture of gray, blue, black, brown, and gold feathers. Roosters have bright blue-green heads with red patches around their eyes. They also have white rings around their necks. Hens are smaller than roosters. They are light brown with cream-colored undersides. Small dark brown and tan spots cover their bodies. Hens have a shorter tail than roosters.

Habitat: farm fields, pastures, prairies, ditches, small wetlands, edges of woodlands

Range: Pheasants live in many parts of North America, including southern Canada. In the United States, pheasants mainly live in midwestern areas. They can live as far south as Texas and New Mexico.

Food: insects, seeds, grains, berries

Nesting: Hens hide their nests in tall grass. They lay 6 to 15 eggs in May or June. The eggs hatch about 24 days later. Chicks grow quickly and can fly in about two weeks.

Behavior: Pheasants usually run if they sense danger. They have powerful leg muscles. But they often flush when there is no other way to escape from predators. Roosters sometimes make a loud crowing sound. They also make a loud cackle when they are alarmed.

GLOSSARY

flush (FLUSH)—to come out of cover; pheasants flush by flying up.

habitat (HAB-uh-tat)—the places and natural conditions in which an animal lives

hybrid (HYE-brid)—the offspring of two different species

safety (SAYF-tee)—a device that prevents a gun from firing

soil erosion (SOYL ee-ROH-zhuhn)—the wearing away of soil by water and wind; soil in a steep area can erode and enter a water source.

species (SPEE-sheez)—a specific type of plant or animal

synthetic (sin-THET-ik)—made by people rather than found in nature

The Great Outdoors—Pheasant Hunting

READ MORE

Lewis, Joan. *Hunting.* Get Going! Hobbies. Chicago: Heinemann Library, 2006.

Wilson, Jef. *Hunting For Fun!* For Fun. Minneapolis, Minn.: Compass Point Books, 2006.

INTERNET SITES

FactHound offers a safe, fun way to find Internet sites related to this book. All of the sites on FactHound have been researched by our staff.

Here's how:

1. Visit *www.facthound.com*

2. Choose your grade level.

3. Type in this book ID **1429608234** for age-appropriate sites. You may also browse subjects by clicking on letters, or by clicking pictures and words.

4. Click on the **Fetch It** button.

FactHound will fetch the best sites for you!

INDEX